W9-CHH-332

W9-CHH-332

ON THE ROAD

Designed and produced by
Aladdin Books Ltd, 70 Old Compton Street, London
W1V 5PA, United Kingdom

Design: David West
          Children's Book Design

Illustrators: Tizzie Knowles, Louise Nevitt, Rob Shone
and Shaun Barlow

Pete Sanders is the head teacher of a North London
primary school, and is working with teachers on
personal, social, and health education.

The publishers would like to thank Seamus, Kimber, Astra, Fiona,
Aminata, Miguel, and all the other children who posed for the
pictures used in this book.

Published in the United States in 1989 by
Gloucester Press, 387 Park Avenue South, New York, NY 10016

ISBN 0-531-17149-3

Library of Congress Catalog
Card Number: 88-83109

Printed in Belgium

ON THE ROAD

PETE SANDERS

GLOUCESTER PRESS
New York · London · Toronto · Sydney

Introduction

When you go out on the road there are many dangers. You share the streets with cyclists, cars, trucks, buses and other pedestrians.

Anybody on the road may cause something to go wrong and accidents can happen to anyone. This book will give you ideas about how to keep safe on the road.

This picture shows a very busy street. Where you live may be much quieter. If you look closely at the picture, you will see things that are designed to help to keep everyone safe. Some of the people are doing things which could be dangerous. Can you spot the dangers? You can check if you noticed them at the end of the book on page 29.

Keeping safe

The streets are full of safety equipment. There are many warning signs for drivers. One kind says schoolchildren are nearby. You have to learn what the pictures on the signs mean.

Traffic lights help to control traffic and people. Many of them have a "walk" sign that lights up. This means that you can cross the road. You should learn the order in which the lights go on and off. You may hear a noise when the lights are green. This is to tell people who cannot see very well that it is safe to cross.

Cars have safety equipment too. For example, there are safety belts to stop people from crashing through the windshield. Can you think of any other car safety devices?

 INFORMATION

This street shows some of the things that keep us safe on the road. It's much safer to cross a road using a footbridge or islands in the middle of the road. But some people ignore these and prefer to take the chance of crossing the road. The road signs tell drivers how fast to go. Bike paths are very useful and it's a shame there aren't more in cities.

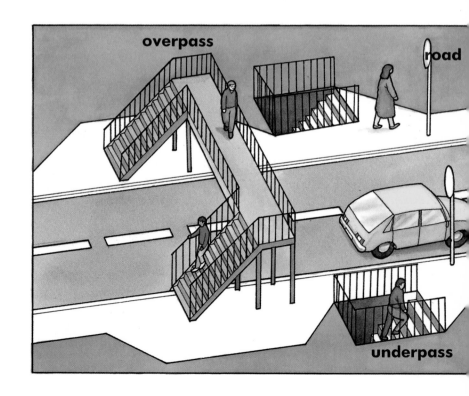

overpass

road

underpass

These boys know that even at crosswalks they have to take care.

islands

bs

bike path

Road signs are usually shaped like rectangles, but a STOP sign is hexagonal. It has large white letters on a red background. Warning signs are usually diamond shaped with black letters on yellow. Other signs can give you important information about traffic. Try to design your own signs.

Safety ideas

Learning about road signs will help you keep safe on the road. But you need to use what you know so that you don't have accidents. If you are walking along a road with no footpath, you should keep to the left hand side of the road, so that you can see the traffic that is coming towards you.

To cross the road safely, remember this simple rule. You have to stop, look and listen and think. If you're in a hurry, you can easily forget to do this. Always take the time to find the safest place to cross a road. This may be at a crosswalk or at a traffic light.

When you're on the streets, it helps if you can be seen easily. That is why some cyclists wear special bands that glow in the dark.

INFORMATION

Crossing the Road
Stop at the edge of the sidewalk. Do not step off it. Now look up and down the street. Use your ears too. Only go across the street if you know you can walk across. You shouldn't have to run! While you are crossing, keep listening and looking. Always cross in a straight line, to get to the other side as quickly as possible.

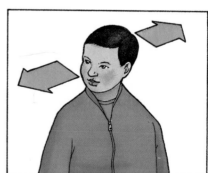
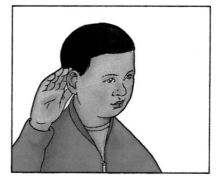

It's a good idea to take your time crossing the road and not rush it.

Road sense

Having road sense can stop accidents. Learning the rules of the road helps you develop road sense. Sometimes rules sound boring. But you need to know why there are rules and what they mean. Without them, games such as volleyball or football would be chaotic. It's the same with the road – everyone has to follow the traffic rules.

Most accidents that happen to children take place very close to where they live because they're not paying attention. Having road sense means always having road safety for yourself and others in mind.

Some people use the street to play ball games. Perhaps you've done this but it's very risky. It's much safer to play in a playground.

PROJECT

Road signs tell you what's ahead and what to be careful of. Make a note of all the signs you see on your way to school. Take a pile of blank cards. Take one card at a time and draw a road sign on it. Spread the cards out. Ask a friend to look at them for 30 seconds. Cover up your signs. See how many of them your friend can remember.

If you're good at skateboarding, practice in the park.

Other road users don't always notice children playing on the sidewalk.

Moving cars

Some drivers aren't as careful as they could be. If a driver isn't concentrating, she or he might do something dangerous, like stopping suddenly or turning without signaling or giving any indication.

When you're walking, you have to allow plenty of space between you and moving cars. This is especially true when it's raining or the road is icy. A fast moving car can skid quite easily and even go onto the pavement. Cars coming out of a driveway may cross the pavement too. Also watch out for cars that are backing up.

If you're a passenger in a car, it's important not to distract the driver. She or he has to concentrate when driving.

INFORMATION

Have you ever tried to cross the street by stepping out between two parked cars? It's difficult to see and be seen if you do this. You may have thought that it was easier than walking to a safer place, but it's much more dangerous. Remember that finding a safer place means being able to see in both directions. Don't try to cross where the road bends.

Never try to cross a highway where cars are traveling very fast.

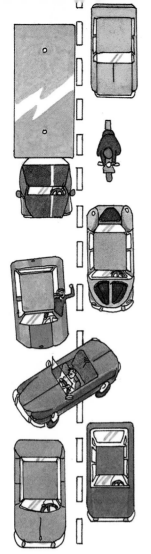

Rush hour

Accidents can happen to anyone at any time. But some times of the day are busier than others and accidents are more likely to happen then. When people are rushing to or from work it is called rush hour.

Everyone has to be particularly careful during rush hour. Many people are in a hurry. Drivers may find it hard to concentrate because there is so much traffic.

Sometimes people don't look when they get out of their car on the street side. This can easily cause an accident. Many cyclists have been knocked down in this way.

People walking on the sidewalk also have to watch out for car drivers. When you are on foot, make sure you're not too near the curb.

PROJECT

Make a list of all the different types of vehicles that use the road. Draw them on the left hand side of a piece of paper. Divide the other side into two columns. Now do a traffic survey: one in the rush hour and one at a quieter time of day. Spend 10 minutes making a mark for each type of vehicle that goes past. What differences did you find?

Being stuck in a traffic jam makes drivers irritable.

They may get out of their car in a way that could hurt a cyclist.

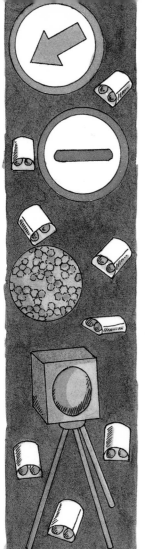

Seeing in the dark

You probably know that it is harder to see and be seen in the dark. Even when roads are well lit, there may be shadows where you can't be noticed. The bad light can play tricks on what drivers are seeing. The glare of another car's headlights sometimes stops drivers from seeing for a few moments.

It's a good idea to be extra careful in the dark. If you are out at night, wear light colors or reflective bands. You may find it useful to have a flashlight with you. If you are on a bicycle, make sure your lights work.

Some roads have objects to show where the middle of the street is. These are rubber pads with reflectors in them. They are called cats' eyes because that is what they look like.

INFORMATION

Light gets in your eyes through the pupil or the middle dark part. The size of the pupil changes according to the amount of light there is. Look in the mirror when a bright light is on. The pupil is smaller so it allows less light in. In dim light your pupil gets larger. When there is very little light, you can't see colors. At night, things seem to be more black and white.

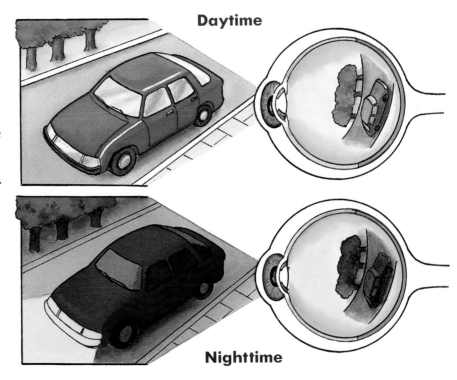

Daytime

Nighttime

You can see how wearing certain colors makes you more visible.

● Do you know which colors can be seen most easily? Here's how to find out.

● Collect a pile of different colored papers.

● Look at them and put them in order of most easily seen to least easily seen.

● Darken the room and check how easy it is to see the colors.

17

Judging distances

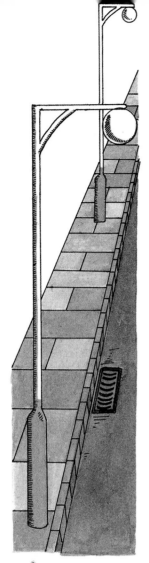

When you cross the road you have to be able to judge exactly how far away cars are. It takes a lot of practice to get this right. Cars that are farther away look smaller than those nearby. Yet it's difficult to tell how far they are if they are moving.

Anyone can make a mistake about how wide a road is too. You might think that you can make it across, but misjudge the distance.

Grown-ups can have problems with distances too. Sometimes you can see cars driving very close to other cars when there is very little traffic.

When you overtake someone on your bike you have to check how far away cars are before pulling out.

PROJECT

Pace out the distance between two lamp posts. How many feet do you think it is? Now measure the distance. How long do you think it will take to walk from one lamp post to the other? Use a watch to see if you judged it correctly. Now try to guess the speed of the cars. Measure the time it takes them to travel between the two lamp posts.

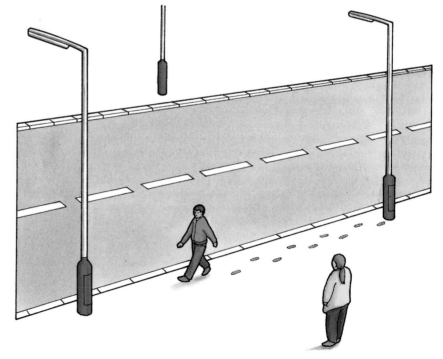

This driver had to stop very quickly because the cyclist misjudged the car's speed.

We can react more or less quickly to things. It depends on how we feel and how tired we are. Test reaction times with a friend. Hold a ruler in one hand. Ask your friend to catch it when you drop it. The part of the ruler your friend catches will show how quick her or his reactions are.

Cycling

Being a good cyclist is a skill that you need to learn. It's best to delay going out on roads until you have had lots of practice. When you feel ready, it's a good idea to go with an adult for the first time.

There are many things to think about when you're out and about on your bike. You need to let other road users know what you are going to do. This means giving clear hand signals. You have to travel on the right part of the road. This is particularly important when you are turning left or passing cars.

All the time you have to think about what other road users might be doing. Remember to think, look and decide what is safe, then signal clearly before you move.

 INFORMATION

Bicycles have to be checked regularly, otherwise they will not work well and may be dangerous. You should oil the chain. The tires should be pumped up to the correct pressure. Check them to see if they are worn and that the valve works. Before you go out, make sure that all the nuts are tight. Test your brakes on a very quiet road or at the playground.

keep bike clean

check brakes

check batteries a
clean lights

don't get oil on
brakes or rim

oil chain

It's best to practice biking in a safe place.

See if you can plan a bicycle test for your friends to try out in a safe place. Here are some of the things you should look out for. How well do they balance? Can they look behind them without wobbling? Do they brake well? How good is their steering? Are their hand signals clear? What do they need to know about traffic rules?

Bike safety

Try not to get into situations where you have to brake suddenly. Slow down gently if you see a hazard. You have to be ready for anything to go wrong on the roads. Apart from the dangers of other road users, the road may be very bumpy, full of potholes, covered with loose gravel or oily.

Always keep your hands near the brake levers. If you do need to stop suddenly, you should use both brakes, but grip the back brake before the front one so that you don't fall off.

Bikes are fairly quiet, so it's all right to use the bell to warn other people that you are there. Lights at night warn others that you are on your bike as well as helping you see.

PROJECT

Test your stopping time on a bike with this simple experiment. You will need two friends, a bike and a stopwatch. Choose a very safe place, such as a park, to try it out. One person has to clap while the other times how long it takes the cyclist to come to a complete standstill. You can take turns doing this. Try it out in different weather conditions.

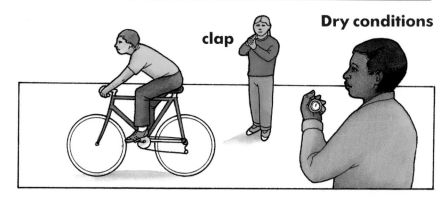

clap — **Dry conditions**

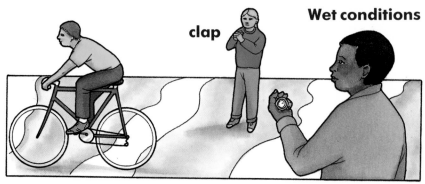

clap — **Wet conditions**

Riding side by side can cause accidents because there isn't enough room for cars.

Dangers to others

Accidents can happen at any time and to anyone. You can help others keep safe if you think about what their needs are. Look out for younger children. They often can't see over parked cars, and sometimes can't be seen by drivers. They are also unpredictable.

Elderly people or those who can't see very well may need help in crossing the street. There may be dangers for them on the sidewalk too. It's easy to trip over cans, bottles and litter of any kind. It's up to us all to put rubbish in cans or take it home with us if there aren't any.

Running or playing on the sidewalk can also be dangerous to people who can't hear well. They may stop suddenly and not realize you're behind them.

INFORMATION

All kinds of people may need help in the street, like the people in the pictures. Can you think of other people who might need help? Have you ever helped someone on the street? What kind of help might these people need? If you do decide to be helpful, be aware of the fact that there are a few people who may look okay but who might harm children.

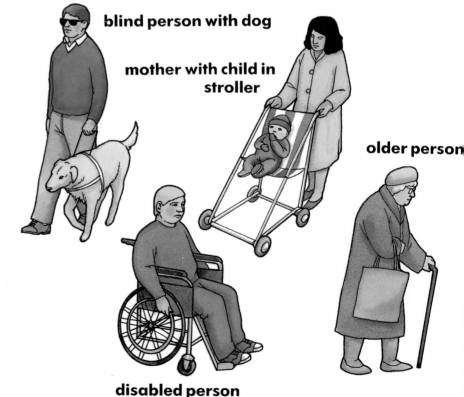

blind person with dog

mother with child in stroller

older person

disabled person

It's best to hold hands with younger children on the street.

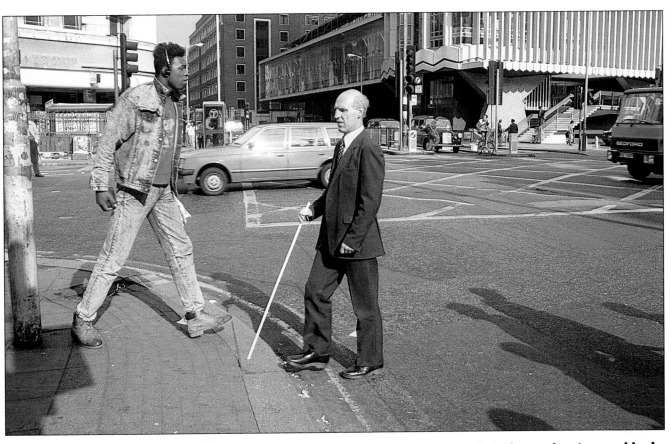

Some blind people may welcome being helped across the road. Others don't need help.

Making yourself safe

Being safe on the road means knowing what the dangers are and learning to avoid them. Be on the lookout all of the time both on the road and on the sidewalk. Remember to walk and not run and to cross the road safely. Learning about danger spots is important. Anywhere the traffic is turning can be risky, as are bends in the road and tops of hills. What other problem places can you think of?

You should use all of the equipment in the street which has been put there to make it less dangerous. For example, some busy roads have a crossing island, where you can wait until it is safe to finish your journey across the street. If you don't take unnecessary risks, you should be safe on the road.

 ## PROJECT

All kinds of ideas and devices are used to help keep you safe on the street. Some of them are shown here. Which ones do you think are the most important? Design a coat of arms, making sure that it has four sections. In each of these spaces you can draw a picture of the street equipment that you think is most important. Get a friend to check it.

WALK and DON'T WALK signs

bike paths

Can you think of any more?

Even the best trained dogs can have accidents. That's why they should be on a leash.

Using an overpass is one of the safest ways to cross a road.

Safety game

Most road accidents happen because people forget to do things, or because they haven't learned the rules of the road in the first place. You can help yourself and others stay safe by making a game which will make them more street wise (see below). But you may have some different ideas. For example, you could make an ABC book of road safety for young children. You can draw a picture which has lots of dangers on it, and get your friends to spot the hazards.

PROJECT

You might want to try out this game. To make it you will need some cardboard, something to draw and color with, some scissors and a ruler. You will need to draw out your board. There's one opposite to give you a few ideas. You can make up your own safety and hazard squares. You can write in your own rules, for example, move back to the start if you cross the road in the wrong place. Instead of using flat counters, you can make little people. Make sure that they are the right size to fit the squares of your board.

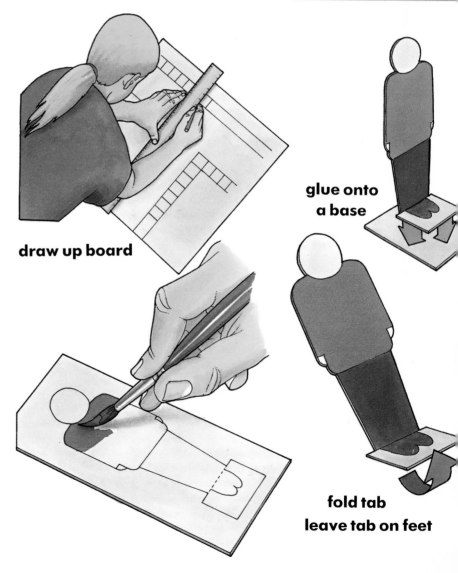

draw up board

glue onto a base

fold tab
leave tab on feet

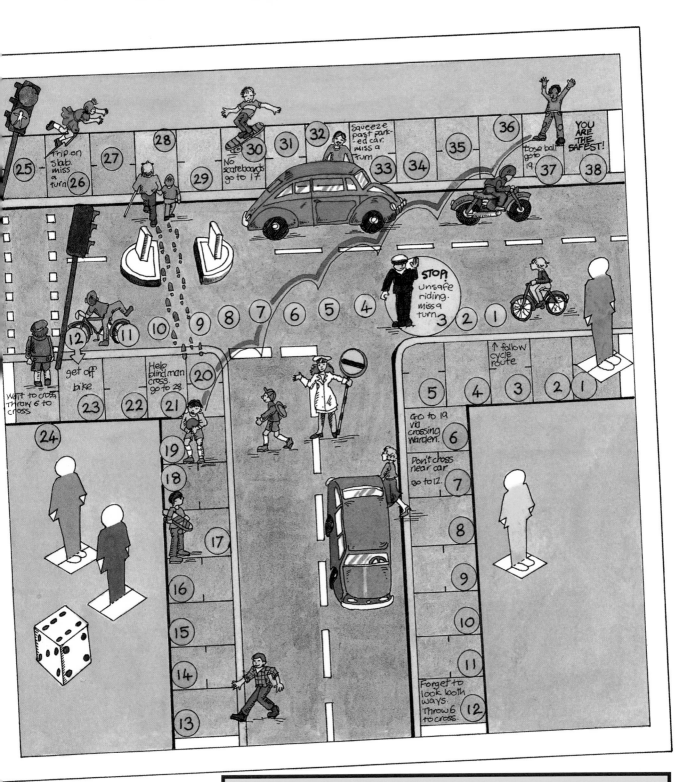

can you think of any other hazards?

Answers to page 4

The children shouldn't be playing with a ball or skateboarding. The boy shouldn't run out into the road with his ice cream. The boy should have his dog on a leash. The car shouldn't be parked on the road. The man should look out for cyclists when he gets out of the car. The sidewalk should be repaired. Can you spot any more?

First Aid

First aid is giving care and help to someone who is hurt. You need to have lessons to be good at first aid. The ideas here are to help you to know what to do if you hurt yourself or if you come across somebody who needs some help. Reading this section does not make you into an expert.

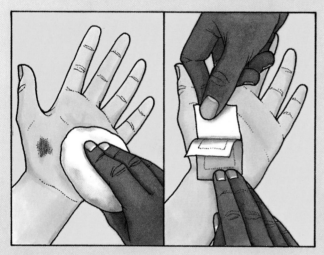

Abrasions

usually happen when the skin slides along a rough surface after a fall. The top layers of the skin are damaged, and this makes it feel very sore. Dirt and grit may have gotten into the wound. Therefore, it needs to be cleaned very carefully. If this is not done properly, an infection may occur. The wound should be covered with a dry dressing.

Crush injuries

can happen in car accidents and on building sites. If people get crushed, they may have damaged the inside of their bodies, as well as the outside, so the most important thing is to contact the ambulance service.

If a crush injury happens on the road, it is the traffic that should be moved around the person. Trying to move the casualty could make things worse. Tight clothing should be loosened, and a light blanket or coat will help to keep the person warm. Crowds should not gather around. If someone is helping already, stay well away.

If you have a crushed finger or toe, bleeding may be going on underneath the skin. Running cold water over the crushed area will help to stop the bleeding. A cold cloth may help too.

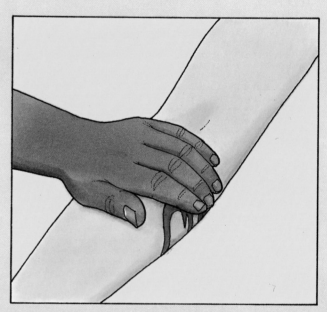

Cuts

If someone has a cut that is still bleeding, pressing on it will stop the flow of blood. Make sure dirt doesn't get into the cut, and cover it with a clean piece of material.

Anybody lying in the street may have passed out. The first thing to do in this case is to get adult help. Putting a light covering over an unconscious person will help them to keep warm. Pay particular attention to hands and feet. People who look like they are asleep should not be moved or given anything to eat or drink.

The recovery position

Laying a person on his or her side may help an accident victim to breathe more easily and may prevent choking. A person trained in first aid knows how to move an injured person.

Car accidents

If a car accident has happened, the first thing to do is to warn other traffic of the dangers, so that nothing worse happens. It's important to remember that traffic can come from both directions.

Some drivers carry a red triangle to warn others. These signs should be placed about 80 feet away from both the front and the back of the vehicles involved. They warn other drivers to slow down.

Emergency

● If you're in an accident, stay calm.
● Make sure you are not in danger.
● Send for help at once.
● Get an adult – maybe another car driver – to use a phone box to dial 911 and call the police.
● If there's no one available, dial 911 and call the police yourself. Remember you don't need any money.

● When someone answers tell them the phone number you are using and explain exactly where you are.
● Tell exactly where the accident has happened, how many vehicles were in the crash and how many people were involved.
● Answer all the questions that the police ask and do not hang up until the person you are talking to has finished.

Index

Photographic Credits:
Cover and pages 11 (both), 13, 19 and 23: Zefa; pages 7, 17,
25 (top), 27 (both): Marie-Helene Bradley; pages 9, 15
(bottom) and 25 (bottom): David Browne; pages 21: ROSPA.